Capitalism

WESLEYAN NEW POETS

Capitalism

Campbell McGrath

Wesleyan University Press
Published by University Press of New England
Hanover and London

For my mother and father and brother
For Elizabeth

WESLEYAN UNIVERSITY PRESS
Published by University Press of New England, Hanover, NH 03755

© 1990 by Campbell McGrath

All rights reserved
Printed in the United States of America   5   4   3   2

∞

Some of these poems previously appeared in *Antaeus, Big Wednesday, Caliban, Kingfisher, Ohio Review, River Styx, Shenandoah, TriQuarterly,* and *Witness.* "What They Ate" and "What They Drank" appeared originally in *The New Yorker.*

The second section of "The Cult of the Individual" has been adapted from the *Journals* of Lewis and Clark.

Excerpt from "Prayers of Steel" in *Cornhuskers* by Carl Sandburg, copyright 1918 by Holt, Rinehart and Winston, Inc. and renewed 1946 by Carl Sandburg, reprinted by permission of Harcourt Brace Jovanovich, Inc.

Lyrics from "Highway to Hell" (Bon Scott, Angus Young, Malcolm Young) © 1979 J. Albert & Son Pty. Ltd. All rights for the U.S. and Canada administered by J. Albert & Son (USA) Inc. Used by permission. All rights reserved. Lyrics from "End of My Line," words and new music adaptation by Woody Guthrie. TRO © Copyright 1963 Ludlow Music, Inc., New York, NY. Used by permission. Lyrics from "Talking Columbia," words and music by Woody Guthrie. TRO © Copyright 1961 (renewed) and 1963 Ludlow Music, Inc., New York, NY. Used by permission.

Library of Congress Cataloging-in-Publication Data

McGrath, Campbell, 1962–
Capitalism / Campbell McGrath.—1st ed.
p.   cm. — (Wesleyan new poets)
ISBN 0-8195-2193-0 — ISBN 0-8195-1195-1 (pbk.)
I. Title. II. Series.
PS3563.C3658C37   1990   89-24962
811'.54—dc20

Contents

Dialectical Poem # 1

The good wood died: hacked, chopped, rent, burnt black,
fried up like bacon. What a forest of symbols that was!
In those days they skied cross-country to school and back,
uphill both ways. Now ashes linger, whitened, fire-black,
koans gilding the upsurge, hang-gliding above what was.

"The Growth of 2nd Stage Timber: An Educational Film." Sure,
but who'll watch—longshoremen? A ship arrives: no one to dock it.
The workers picket for better wages, hours, health insurance:
the union man says we'll see, but can't be sure.
Meanwhile, the labor board strikes workers' claims from the docket!

But the wood was hewn to make a ship: ghost-white ashes
serve the mariner as stars. Scabs and strikers collide/merge:
just as historical opposites form a new whole, a clash
without residue of death. *There's no such thing as ashes.*
Stars, timber, ships, men: all manner of destinies converge.

One
Capitalism

My friends are gonna be there too
—AC/DC, "Highway to Hell"

Sunrise and Moonfall, Rosarito Beach

What I remember of Mexico
is how the glass apple of mescal glowed
and exploded like a globe of seeds
or something we couldn't pronounce
or know the secret name of, never,
and even when the federales shook us down for twenty bucks
as they must, to save face,
I couldn't lose the curve and rupture
of that sphere—half-full, hand-blown, imperfect
as our planet. Sure, everything is blowing open
now, all the freeways and skinheads, the music
invisibly blasting, radio waves invading the spines and craniums
of all this. San Diego, Tijuana, the Beach of Dead Dogs
where we slept in the cold, local kids incredulous
of Ed up early for no reason
driving golf balls out into the restlessly pounding surf.
Jesus, we're always hitting golf balls. It seems to be
some irreducible trait. There's Rob smashing the plaster icons,
all the bleeding martyrs and aqua pigs
and pink squinting Virgins the radiant chapel of candles
induced us to need. Jesus, let me ask, please,
before he decapitates you also with a wicked six-iron slice,
why are we always the ones on the beach
as dawn sucks the last drops from mescaline shards,
the ones who beat the sacred iguanas to death
as the sun comes right up
and the shadow-globe finally dances off stage,
the moon, I mean,
that other white world of men
driving golf balls to seas of dust and oblivion—
chrome-headed, flag-waving, violent, American.

Silt, Colorado

The night crossing—empty ski towns, mining towns, full moon on the light snow and Mike asleep since Denver. Dawn came over the mountains behind us and the west appeared slowly out of the winter air. To describe Silt would require a tactile vocabulary to match the roiling high country, purple and dusk fading down from the peaks: long grazing plateaus above the river, savage dun-pale pastels, the cliffs, gulch and guyot, each shade, each stone itself. Five horses walked through tall grass down to the young Colorado River to drink—the ice was breaking up, mist was rising from the water.

Then the long pull—Martian Utah, sad Las Vegas, the ponderous, mesquite-crazed Mojave, Baker, Barstow, Los Angeles. In Barstow I stopped for a cup of coffee. After ten minutes at the red counter the waitress asked us all to leave. The kitchen was on fire and our coffee was free. Looking back through the plate-glass window I saw pies in the rack: apple, cherry, coconut cream, lemon meringue. Mike sat up and his hair was splayed with sleep as the fire engines raced past us into the parking lot. That was Barstow. Silt is beyond me.

Rifle, Colorado

I doubt they were used to strangers in the Rifle Cafe, wrapping their sausage in pancakes a little after dawn. I think the earnest woman frying eggs and the girl in the cowboy hat tracing her finger through spilled flour were mother and daughter. I doubt the lined man drinking bourbon at the bar was either father or brother. I don't know where the guides would lead their parties to hunt for bighorn and whitetail that day. I don't know how often they came to the cafe, or what they thought about, or what they ate. I don't know what their names were, where they lived, whether their families raised cattle or horses or stayed in bed in the morning.

I do know that there were cowboy hats and dirty orange workmen's gloves, the coffee was strong, the pancakes were good, Main Street was gravel, the river ran by, the sun rose just as we got there, night left the Rockies reluctantly, snow and timber diminished in daylight, the mountains emerged slowly with dawn—high country in winter is beautiful and lonely.

Capitalist Poem #5

I was at the 7-11.
I ate a burrito.
I drank a Slurpee.
I was tired.
It was late, after work—washing dishes.
The burrito was good.
I had another.

I did it every day for a week.
I did it every day for a month.

To cook a burrito you tear off the plastic wrapper.
You push button #3 on the microwave.
Burritos are large, small, or medium.
Red or green chili peppers.
Beef or bean or both.
There are 7-11's all across the nation.

On the way out I bought a quart of beer for $1.39.
I was aware of social injustice

in only the vaguest possible way.

Where the Water Runs Down

1

High Country Crags and Moon, Sunrise

In Ansel Adams' photograph the moon disintegrates
like sandstone. The inverted V of cliff in shadow
and the chevron of dark sky nearly meet
to consume the crest
of carefully delineated sunlight along the ridge.
This clarity signals a vision
without mitigation. It is a pure, chromatic world,
a landscape where ideas dominate facts
as light determines exposure.

Dry pines along her flanks. Douglas fir and juniper
remain hidden in the deeper arroyos.

In the next frame *Aspens,*
Dawn, Dolores River Canyon
become wardens of an Emersonian ideal,
light thrown scintillant off edges and spires like needles
or a wave towing zones of sure and distinct tonality
down a slope of boulders and loose scree,
a tragic quality to the shadows of the transcendent grove,
until each white-fingered branch, each dew-glazed bud,
is lit from within.

2

> *Oregon State is mighty fine*
> *If you're hooked on to the power line*©
> —Woody Guthrie

What Woody Guthrie leaves out of his song
about the Grand Coulee Dam
is not the flumed bulk
shouldering clouds and mountains aside.
Neither is it the beauty of the black river;

the smell of horses in rain in the wild gorge country;
the catalogue of states gripped by dust and Depression—
Texas, Oklahoma, Kansas, Georgia, Tennessee;
nor even the old desire to tame the wilderness,
to shape river and mountain and desert to man's will.
What's never mentioned, left unsung,
is the nature of that time
when a dam was something to sing about—
an attitude of profound wonder, honed by despair,
humming through high-tension wires
all across the country,
technology's promise
brought to every town and ranch and farm—not only
along the sinuous Columbia choked with logs,
but everywhere, all over this land, from California
to the New York Island. An era
finding voice in a song about *e-leca-tri-cy-tee.*
A vast, implicit history, east and west,
growth and opportunity and inequality,
crystalline in the moment—
just as a hologram, when shattered, retains
the image of the whole in every shard and fragment—
from Maine to Oregon,
from Plymouth Rock to the Grand Coulee Dam,
where the water runs down.

3

                        What Ansel Adams leaves out
is neither song, stone, nor innuendo
of light cascading through rain-laced aspens.
Lost at the base of Blanca Peak
are two figures: one pulls up stakes
while the other stirs a pot of coffee with a tin spoon.
They hike all day along the ridge-line,
and at evening make camp in a valley

where a thin stream is marked by alder
and gooseberries. They build a fire
to cook macaroni and cheese, and heat cans of beans
in the coals for dinner. Late at night,
in contrast to all rules of composition,
they beat a riven, smoldering log with pine boughs,
sending sparks like clouds and flocks of birds
and winter storm in the valley
rising up to the stars, splinters of light or stone,
innumerable and inseparable.

Memphis

Were we in town for the Elvis to-do? *We sure were.* Did we go to the midnight vigil last night? *We sure did.* How did we all like it? *Wonderful.* Every time she went there she got chills. *We knew what she meant.* She thinks Graceland is about the most moving place she ever was. Just looking at all those things, knowing they were his things, like the cup he drank out of, the mirror he looked into, his little fuzzy pillows, his toothbrush. It was a shame. He would of only been 50 years old this year, too. He was the King, though, he surely was. . . . Well, did we like our catfish? *You bet.* More coffee? *No thanks.* Y'all have a nice time in Memphis now. *We will.*

In fact, we had a miserable time. We drove all day and night and day again to get there from L.A. Albuquerque was a net of lights, magnificently purple in the first tinting of dawn. You slide down into its web from the high plains, then back into mountains. And Arkansas at night, picking up the fringe of some tropical storm system, wipers singing that blue tune, coffee from truck stops and 7-11's, Woody Guthrie and Black Flag and Elvis on the walkman. We slept in the car, with Charlie's surfboard tied to the roof, in the parking lot across the street from green-and-orange-lit Graceland, after the other six thousand mourners left the gates. All those candles, and flower hearts, and women in raincoats crying, hysterical women with bright lipstick, and their husbands in toupees—from his hometown too, Tupelo, Mississippi—and troops of women sweeping rose petals into the gutter afterwards, members of the Elvis Fan Club, Memphis Chapter, as we tried to sleep in the stifling humidity, the drone of rain and mosquitoes.

In the morning we fought our way into the very first tour group. All I remember is how small-time the place seemed, just a country house, really, the almost pathetic homeliness of it. No guitar-shaped pool, no solid-gold Cadillac. Just the TV he always watched while he ate. A statue he gave to his mama. Racks of spangled, American eagle jumpsuits. We left town right afterwards. Rain all the way home through Tennessee, the tangled hills of Virginia, the storm building up to hurricane strength, past the terrible battlefield at Shiloh, and later Bull Run, places where Americans died in a roar of musket fire, all night through the relentless weather, Hurricane Elvis we call it, until even coffee won't do, or the sad songs of dust, Woody Guthrie singing about the Grand Coulee Dam, Johnny Cash with "Folsom Prison Blues," long miles of rain in the Appalachian night, dirges for the fallen, and into Washington as grey light broke from the east.

Los Angeles

One time in L.A. we ate some acid and went down to the cliffs to hit golf balls into the ocean. We said a patch of kelp way out was the green, surrounded by black rocks and waves. Ed was driving like a pro, three hundred yards, straight as an arrow. After a while we climbed down the cliff. We threw golf balls at each other which bounced around in the holes and crazy blue rocks, and rolled into the little pools of water. The sun was going down over Catalina, and the light in the breaking waves was beautiful, all refracted colors, green and purple and orange. I stood on a rock and a wave soaked me. Charlie sat up high on a spur in dark glasses and a Hawaiian shirt. Rob ran out onto dangerous points to hit some irons. He had to race back in front of giant tangerine waves. All the faces and the dinosaur bones in the cliffs came out like blue and yellow amoebas. When we went to find the golf balls in the tide pools they had been swallowed by anemones. You could see them disappearing down their gullets. The tide was coming in fast. We laughed like hell at the bugs buzzing around our heads. There were bugs, weren't there? It was time to go.

Dave drove us home. On the way Rob could see the layers of stars, like transparencies laid one over the other to show the biology of a frog. Ed saw a different animal every block. "You guys saw the peacocks, right?" Dave decided to take a *new route,* find a *new way,* blaze a *new trail* through the twisting back streets of Palos Verdes. Somehow we ended up at the 7-11 on the corner, and Mark picked up a twelve-pack of Old Milwaukee. At home, in the driveway, we smelled smoke. Jesus, the engine's burning up. Or else oranges, exploding on the roof. Wet orange-smoke in the air. Who's throwing oranges? The neighbors will hear. We went inside, down to the basement to watch the VCR. Mark put on Gumby and Pokey and I almost lost my mind. The big race to Thimble Corners. Only Pokey ran into a book, right into the story, with cowboys and Indians. Dinosaurs roll up into balls and come back as a stagecoach. They'll never make it to Thimble Corners in time for the glass of lemonade. The baseball went right through Gumby's head. Watch out, Gumby, here comes the Missile Bird! The terrible, terrible Missile Bird. After that we watched "Rock and Roll High School," "Videodrome," "Altered States," and "Apocalypse Now." Everything was cool except when I thought the salt water soaking my groin was blood. For a while I worried about the police helicopter scanning the backyard with its spotlight. Mark used the remocon to freeze the picture, run it backwards, speed it up. Dave loved it when William Hurt drank iguana blood. I wanted to go to the kitchen. I met Ed on the stairs. "Don't go upstairs. There's dead animals up there."

Dawn finally came, and thick dew on the grass and the fallen fruit of the lemon tree in the wet green grass. The cats appeared from somewhere, warm and hungry. Nobody fed them yesterday. I was alone in the backyard with the cats. Everyone was asleep inside. The TV was still on, rerunning movies, and I could hear the Ramones banging out "Rockaway Beach." I was alone in the backyard. I was alone with the cats, and the wet grass, and the deflated basketball, and the fallen oranges and lemons, and the eucalyptus tree, and the birds, and the rising sun.

Langdon, North Dakota

Just across the Red River of the North we pulled over at dusk to watch a farm auction near Langdon, North Dakota. Pickup trucks were parked for a quarter mile in either direction. Wind shook the waist-high grass and weeds, lifting conic sections of dust swirling into the white, slanting, late-summer sunlight. As we came into the yard crowded with farmers and farmers' wives and children the family guns were on the block: shotguns, deer rifles, down to a bolt-action .22, "just right for a youngster." By the barn, Charlie deciphered a family history in farm equipment: '41 tractor, '51 truck and spreader, '72 tractor, '78 combine—good times and fallow, all going. The auctioneer was a friend from the next county, and the women laughed softly at his jokes, self-consciously, caught somewhere between a wake and a square dance, while the farmers smiled then gazed off into the trees as if listening to the wind. It was a wind that pulled the auctioneer's words from his mouth and left him working his jaws broadly and soundlessly, a grey-haired man in a cowboy hat waving his arms while the buzz of grasshoppers from the endless fields and the noise of thrashing leaves roared and roared. It was a dry, hard wind that blew until it was the sound of the citizens of Langdon singing hymns in the one-story Lutheran church at the edge of town, as their forebears had offered up prayers of thanks a hundred years earlier at the first sight of the borderless grasslands, moving west in the curl of the great human wave of migration, Swedes and Norwegians off the boats from Oslo or Narvik or Trondheim, sent out by train to the home of relatives in Chicago—an uncle whose pickling plant already bore the promise of great wealth—and on north and west, some falling out among the prosperous lakes of Wisconsin, the meadows and pinewoods of Minnesota, the white birch forests like home and the green hills like heaven, through the last of the moraine and glacial defiles, across the lithe Mississippi and into the edge of the vast prairie, the Great Plains of North America still raw with Sioux and locust plagues, the last massive buffalo hunts flashing in the hills of Montana no more than a generation gone, the Arctic wind massing a thousand miles to the north and barrelling down the continent, along the width and breadth of grass, the Dakotas, Nebraska, sod and wild flax in the spring, limitless land, a place to plant and sow that neither Indians nor winters fierce as Stockholm's nor the virulent range wars could take away from the Vorlegs and Johannsens and Lindstroms, a tide of settlers moving out across the heartland, naming lakes for Icelandic heroes, founding towns like Fertile and Walhalla, islands in the great grass delta. It was the sweet wind of Capitalism in the inland Sargasso.

The auction began at noon, was almost over when we arrived. Gone already were the canoe, wading pool, camper, motorcycles, lawn furniture, toys, old clothes, the house, the land itself. Through the window I could see a stag's head over the mantel. Charlie's boots were thick with dust. As we left they were auctioning off an artificial Christmas tree, a last-ditch offering from Sears or Woolworth's. "A real handy article, folks, only gotta wait four months to get your money's worth—do I hear a dollar, do I hear four bits?"

It is nearing the day the smiling auctioneer spoke of, that promised Christmas, a season of hope and redemption. I have carried the draggled plastic tree across the continent and back in my heart. I have felt the silvered needles sting, heard them rustle in the glow of blinking Christmas lights like wheatfields in the first wind of autumn. It is a wind which carries the seeds of life and the dust of extinction. I have dreamt of tinsel and glass balls, of a living room in the heart of the Great Plains. It is a winnowing wind. It is a bitter wind.

Capitalist Poem #7

I stole the UNICEF box.
I didn't mean to.
It was an accident.
I didn't turn it in at school.
I wanted it.
I kept it.
I hid it in my closet.

The box grew on my mind every day.
I thought of what it would buy for the Africans.
Four schoolbooks.
A dozen meals.
Eighty-five polio vaccinations.
Nine hundred million vitamin tablets.

Eventually I think I blew all the money at 7-11.
Some friends came with me and we splurged.

We bought: Chunkies, Big Buddies, baseball cards,
M&M's, Charleston Chews, fire balls, rootbeer barrels,
Clark Bars, Snickers, Milky Ways, bubble gum,
Sweet 'n' Sours, Red Hots, Marathon Bars, and Pixie Stix.

To be perfectly honest, I might have gotten that money one year at Christmas when my best friend Bobby Wixam broke both his legs sledding. I was OK, even though I was on the sled too when we ran into the light pole. But it was Bobby's birthday, either that day or the next, and the party favors were sets of little blue dinosaurs which I really wanted. They actually looked more like a pack of prehistoric dogs, or wolves. And on Sunday his dad was going to take us to the Redskins game. But when Bobby broke his legs we couldn't go. Everything was cancelled. I was so disappointed that my mother gave me five dollars.

I don't really remember what happened to the UNICEF box.
I might have lost it.

What They Ate

All manner of fowl and wild game: venison, raccoon, opossum, turkey.
Abundant fishes, excepting salmon, which ws. found distasteful.
Meat of all sorts, especially pig, which roamed free and was fatty.
Also shellfish: quahogs and foot-long oysters; lobster, though considered
   wasteful.

Wild fruit: huckle and rasp, blue being known as "skycolored" berries.
Parsnips, turnips, carrots, onions: these sown loosely and rooted out;
while these were cultivated in orchards: apples, peaches, apricots,
   cherries.
Cabbage—favored by the Dutch as *koolslaa,* by the Germans as
   sauerkraut—

was boiled with herbs brought from England; thyme, hyssop, marjoram,
   parsley.
Pumpkin, dried, or mashed with butter, where yams grew sparsely.
Corn, with beans as *succotash;* called *samp* when milled to grist;
in the South, hulled and broken, as *hominy;* or fried with bacon as grits.
Maple ws. not favored; loaves of white sugar worth considerable money
were kept under lock, cut with special sugar shears. For honey,

bees were imported, called "English flies" by the Narragansett.

What They Drank

Water, rarely. Sometimes goat's milk, later cow's. Never coffee or tea:
too expensive to import.
Liquor reigned: flagons of ale, casks and demijohns of fine French
      brandy,
costly decanters of Spanish port,

all laboriously shipped or smuggled, until at last the miracle grain
of the New World, corn,
was mashed and fermented into whiskey at great pecuniary gain.
Thus was born

our second-oldest industry: distilling. Though the wild Concord grape
      lacked
flavor, breweries spread withal;
the growth of orchards led to cider and applejack,
peach brandy in the South a windfall.

Also popular were mixed drinks: cider & rum, cider & mead,
above all *flip,* being beer
sweetened with molasses or pumpkin, fortified with spirit alcohol as
      needed,
then scalded with a hot poker.

Lastly came rum from the Indies, called "kill-devil" by the Dutch,
      Manhattan awash
with the diabolical liquor,
said worse even than gin: worse for the poor because cheaper, worse
for the rich because quicker.

Berlin

It's midnight. Berlin. You're in the Burger King and a man is threatening you with a chair. He's holding it above his head, up almost to the ceiling. It seems he's mad because you're Irish. His buddies from the London rugby club are with him. A free and independent Ireland, you explain. A free and independent . . . But he's a statue. He's Atlas, frozen in mid-swing. It was one of those new, upscale fast-food places, with fake marble counters, and a salad bar with golden bowls of lettuce and chick-peas and croutons, a little gold-handled ladle for your 1,000 Island dressing. There was nobody there but us and them. Dave was drinking a milk shake. Atlas' friends were looking a little vague. Ed kept staring at him. Atlas put the chair down.

Out into the night of stars. Comets rising like angelfish, moving in luminous schools to the horizon, a taste like cinnamon or rivers of dust where the faint metal clang of the moon on your tongue is a memory of the black desert and Las Vegas shimmering in the center, neon pearl in the oyster of human misery. After a minute you realize you have your sunglasses on. You can't even see the stars. It's the million lights of the Kurfürstendamm, white and yellow like poppies. The glasses filter an aluminum brilliance of green, walls exploding with brassy suns. German kids in boots and varsity jackets cruise by on skateboards. "Cool, daddy-o!" We run into our friend Klaus the Cowboy. "I like the cowboys of Texas and Wyoming and Ohio. Like Buddy Holly and Gene Vincent. Only, my friend tells me that there is no heroin in Wyoming, and so I am not sure that I could live there." Shooting up with friends in the kitchen. Dozing in the park all afternoon. They can't catch you. You'll never get hooked. You can always wander down to the tin-pony rodeo or swim off into the night, another angel in the fishbowl eating rubber worms or dog food or scraps of Whoppers out of trash cans, whatever bait they're using for billionaire catfish that season. Planets are screaming like blue eyes. They can't catch you. The moon kicks down your door. Stars rush in like piranha.

Capitalist Poem #19

With all the lovely Mikes and Judys from La Habra and Mission Viejo winning cash and prizes on "Sale of the Century" and "The Price Is Right" five days a week, with all the Pats and Debbies from Encino finding their "Love Connection" with Chuck Woolery every afternoon at 4:30, and taking into account the total number of spins of the "Wheel of Fortune," it seems that by this time everyone in L.A. must be a lucky winner. It seems that everyone in all of Southern California must have felt the touch of the mysterious hand of beneficence. Each little homemaker in Valencia has received silver flatware or a new dryer or the La-Z-Boy reclining love seat, each computer programmer in Burbank has accepted the keys to a brand-new Olds Cutlass Classic—for each security guard a year's supply of dog food, for each bank teller a wood-burning stove, which isn't much use here, admittedly, but it's better than nothing, and anyway she won it, and he won his, and the guy next door won his too. They all won! Their two-day winnings total eleven thousand three hundred and eighty-four dollars! And all that sun, the sea. We've even turned the basement into an entertainment center with a large-screen TV and a fruit-juice bar for the kids. America, America.

But even though it seems that way you know it isn't true. They can't all win. What kind of game is it where everybody wins? Sure, there's the trip to historic Mexico, but someone has to pick Door #2. Behind Door #2 is a man with an ice pick who will stab you in the eye and then sodomize your dead body. Behind Door #1 was a world of perfect happiness and understanding, a world designed by the winners of beauty pageants across the country, but you traded Door #1 for the right to see what's in the box. What is in the box? A meadow in the Rocky Mountains so beautiful at midnight that deer moving near the salt lick make you think of angels. A dust storm near Pocatello, Idaho, which stains the very sky red above the Snake River, yellow combines moving on the horizon like horsemen in surreal snow, newsreel footage of the Dust Bowl with lines of tired and despairing men in Kansas City or Tulsa, waiting for a bowl of soup and some bread, just enough to keep them going. It's true. They can't all win. Not just in Oklahoma, or Redondo Beach, not just in America. They can't all win anywhere. For every Toni and Ted there's got to be a Kim, and you've been in the car with her when she stopped at Mr. Ricky's Liquor to buy "the load," after all she does her best work on the load, and only twenty bucks for all those pills and so much easier than slamming pins. We're not even talking about Renaldo, or the black guys hanging around out front hitting the bus-stop sign with a Wiffle-ball bat, or Mr. Ricky, if there is a Mr. Ricky. Because the fun never stops. At Ed's house in Long Beach you start right in with breakfast. Everyone jumps in the car and you drive forty-five minutes to your favorite fried-chicken place, and you wash it down with cold duck and malt liquor and spend the rest of the day driving pointlessly around boulevards, palm trees, 7-11's, maybe hit the beach for a little while before heading to the Goose where it's happy hour all day, two girls on stage at all times, and cable sports on the large-screen TV's in the corner. If you get sick of the music you can always play Mr. Do. But the next day you wake up with a hangover and get scared when you remember that life is boring, that sex and violence are fun or at least interesting, like masturbating to ZZ Top videos, like when you picked up that chick at the mall and took her home and pulled the train, "a fat white chick," as Rob says, who worked at McDonald's and didn't remember too clearly the next day but thanked you and she had toy soldiers in her pocket which you wondered at but she said they were for her kids three girls Pammi six Traci four Joann two and a half which explained it. No, you weren't exactly proud of yourself, but it was a good story and pretty funny really.

But who's to say that hand won't someday reach down gently to tap them all with its Midas touch, money from the sky, a chance to climb the pyramid of commodities, turning their whole life golden, magical, an almost sexual gratitude at the wonder of it. A touch soft as a kiss, but so much more! Everything's different now. Things are going to be fine from here on in.

Still, my favorite story is Mark's one about Joe Bosconi. Joe Bosconi was the poorest guy in school. His clothes were from K Mart and were always too old and too small and smelled bad. When you went to his house for his birthday party and played party games the prize for the winner was a nickel. His grandmother sat in the living room in a wheelchair chain-smoking Camels. And when Joe Bosconi's family won the state lottery—not $50,000-a-year-for-life, but enough, a stake, a second chance—they bought two snowmobiles and a camper.

Capitalist Poem #22

The waves roll in from the boiling depths. Tangled mats of seaweed, rotting vegetation and dead fish, a deadly turbulence of greys and purples and browns. Past the reef the wild breakers, foaming like unbridled mustangs, resolve back to azure, the scattered watery-orange of coral heads, and in the shallows marked by deep green shoals a creature rises to the surface. Water falls in torrents as it rears up on its hind legs and bellows. How to describe that unearthly shriek! Palm trees bend flat to the ground in the wind of its passage. The fishermen's bamboo huts collapse like pick-up sticks. Miles away the earth rumbles and mud slides block railroads and highways. Finally, immense and magisterial, shaking its baggy, tendrilous hide like a sort of stringy blue throw rug, and shooting mysterious rays from its eyes, the creature moves inland in search of major population centers and small boys in baseball caps.

Thus the Heavy Metal Monster is born, creature of fire and water, ravager of farmstead and city alike. But just when you think you've seen this one before and wonder what else is on (nothing but cartoons and a nature show about the rain forest of West Africa), something really strange happens. The Monster unzips its shaggy skin and out jumps David Lee Roth, much bigger than life, in dark glasses and a peppermint-stick jumpsuit, and the camera zooms in to show us the really hot chain-and-leather-clad vixens crying out for more punishment, and more, and faster, and the guys in the band standing around in eye makeup with lots of flames. And before we know it the flames have engulfed Yokohama and are heading straight for Tokyo! And before we can grasp what's happening, the Monster, a sinister product of industrial pollution and the corrupt morals of dancing teenagers, takes advantage of the greed and incompetence of assorted Generals and government leaders to ravage the entire nation, but in the end is vaporized by a clever stratagem of the bespectacled old timer and his precocious grandchildren. *Ah! Ooah?! Good jumping there. A success!* And now we realize that we have seen this one, but before we can change the channel somebody pipes up with the idea that we've taken the Monster too literally, we've misinterpreted this gargantuan image risen from the sea. And even though we don't know who this guy is, and he certainly wasn't invited to the party, he goes on to suggest that the Monster is a symbolic represen- tation of American popular culture, thus its association with things new and dangerous, technology and rock and roll, and its ultimate defeat by the caretakers of traditional Japanese culture. And he goes on to cite numerous other examples we all remember well. The Air Force guys in Amsterdam who dropped acid and went to see *Purple Rain* hour after hour, day after day. The Arab kid in the Redskins jacket we met on the train coming back to Tunis from the ruins of Carthage. And the carousel in that Spanish fishing village where Elizabeth and I basked over beers and *tapas* for days, the fishermen hauling their great baskets of squid and purple octopi to market while the swallows swooped over the harbor at dusk when the carousel lit up and music played and everything began to spin—and though we were the only ones in town to know it, those emblems painted on the outer rim of the merry-go-round, the figured wheel flashing pink and green, were the logos of Batman, Superman, Spiderman and the Avengers. As the coins of the Spanish in another era, the fabled pieces of eight, so David Lee Roth. As the highways of the Romans, so Liberace, so Mickey Mouse, so James Dean.

So the party goes on, and it doesn't really matter what we watch, because all we're interested in is more punishment, and more, and faster—and could you turn the volume up please! But at exactly that moment, just as David Lee hits the really cool part, I remember something I saw on that nature show about the creatures of the rain forest, the nectar-sucking bats, and the giant sloths, and the harlequin butterflies. In all the diversity of insect life— termites and grubs, leaf-cutter ants, the warriors and the queens—they showed one ant in the midst of a strange seizure, a kind of stiff-legged dance. It had inhaled the miscroscopic spore of a parasitical fungus. The fungus travels to the ant's brain and takes control of its nervous system. Abandoning the forest floor for the first time in its life, the ant selects a tree of a certain species and begins to climb. When it reaches the top it sinks its mandibles into a green shoot and dies. The fungus then enters the tree, its natural host, through the holes the ant has bitten, where it resumes its natural life cycle. In time the fungus consumes the ant's entire body, leaving a withered, mummified corpse. I also remember, in an interview, how David Lee Roth's parents viewed their son's career. They told how, as a child, David Lee was prone to strange outbursts, a period when he would bang his spoon and shout and roll on the floor. Dinner guests looked on in alarm until his parents would explain: "Don't worry—this is just David Lee's monkey hour." And at that point David Lee interrupted their response to say: "Yeah. Now my whole life is monkey hour and I make millions of dollars for it."

Negril Beach, Jamaica

Saturday nights in those west Jamaican towns between the Blue Mountains and the sea, people seem to spring from the earth, direct from the dirt of poverty, from the coves and valleys, the cane fields, the jungle, the mud flats along the Green and Maggotty Rivers. The night itself is blue with life in Lucea, Little London, Savanna-la-Mar, girls in white dresses and their young men in neatly mended shirts, their modesty amidst profusion, the wild growth of bougainvillaea, jelly coconuts overhead, yellow planets in orbit, the simple fact of poverty like the fact of wild bananas in the hills—a ubiquitous native vegetation. In the mountainous rain forest, survival is a history of competitive growth. Whenever a break occurs in the canopy, seedlings and saplings race for the gap to the life-sustaining sun, the winner eventually rising hundreds of feet, filling the hole, *accessing the window of opportunity*—leaving the rest to wither and die in the shade. An unusual side effect of this frantic renewal cycle is the lack of an adequate root system. Survival at the heights is tenuous. Even the largest of rain-forest trees may be felled by a strong wind, creating a domino effect of other toppled giants, each of whom had relied on its neighbor for support, tearing an even larger hole in the canopy, a new break for sunlight to enter, a new chance for furious, doomed, competitive growth.

My family used to go to Jamaica over Christmas, to Negril, where we rented a little cinder-block house something like a suburban garage, with a maid, cook, and gardener. Besides the obvious issues of cultural imperialism there was sun, azure water, and seven miles of beautiful sandy beach. There was one time—it was Boxing Day, when all the local families come to the beach, all the little Jamaican kids, five and eight to a family, laughing and playing in the water—I think it was our third year there. My brother and I were out swimming when Oswald, the octogenarian beach guard, started hollering about something or other. Our father was talking to him. Two little kids were there, and their friend was swimming and now he wasn't. Dad came running down and we started thrashing around looking for something, the missing friend, the body, which there obviously wasn't one of, this being vacation, the Christmas season, Jamaica. Which is when the two little kids started calling from the shallows—here he is, here he is. Well pick him up for Godsakes. But they're too scared and I rush over and there he is, face down, very thin, maybe twelve years old, a scuba mask filled with water and foam around his lips, limp, heavier than he looks, like something filled with sand, as I carry him out of the surf, running up the beach, pulling his mask off, Dad running over, turn him around, pump his chest, let's go, come on breathe, but of course he won't, by this time a big circle of onlookers, the Rastas taking charge—give the man room—and after a few minutes the father and two sisters show up, weeping, hanging back at the edge of the circle, remote, private in their grief, and that was the end of it. Eventually the police came and took him away in a jeep. I remember there was a little note about it in the *Weekly Gleaner,* how the American doctor administered treatment to no avail, the concerned officials, the bereaved family, one of three drownings over the holidays. His name was Dalton Johnston.

Meanwhile reggae from the numerous cool spots floats rythmically out to sea and herons swoop low across the water. Night has fallen, and the fishermen in their ancient dugouts paddling steadily towards the reef look back at the lights coming on along the great half-moon sweep of beach. Leaving the murmurous ganja smoke of Eli's Uprising Shack after midnight, a crazed desire for bananas sends you and your brother, laughing wildly, deep into the jungle. But you can't find any bananas, the thick green bunches suspended in darkness, safely invisible in the maze of shadows. You're about to turn back when you stagger out into the new clearing where the trees fell in the storm last week, vastly changed, luminous in moonlight, already dense with a growth of waist-high trees and the gleaming, hooded eyes of dozens of white orchids.

Miami

Banking in to the Miami airport
I saw traffic like a river of light,
2000 matching houses, refineries,
parking lots with new cars by the acre,
a grid, a city of streets,
the red signs of restaurants,
strong boulevards shouldering
the burden, the avenues, the mark
of a million people.

The runway lights
are blue and green.
O! the runway lights
are blue, green.

Capitalist Poem #23

We roamed the city like tumbling tumbleweeds. We drove the streets of Long Beach in search of something vital and new. The chili nachos at 7-11 were good but we wanted more, we wanted it all, we wanted *everything*. After a while we gave up and headed home. Things were on TV. Ed says he knows this guy in Anaheim. Mark wants to watch the show about Melanesia, cannibalism and cargo cults, airstrips in the jungle where the natives still await the return of the miraculous commodity gods. The gingko, we learn, is a prehistoric tree, the last of its kind, a living fossil. The last king of Fiji ate humans whenever possible—*long pig* was the islanders' term for the delicacy. This is where we live, the city of Long Pig, California. We worship commodities dropped from the sky. Ed pops a beer. The sun disappears like the archangel of smog. The oil pumps say *wicky wicky*. Everyone seems pretty excited, pretty sure that this is it. Charlie calls the operator in Suva. "Is this Fiji? We hate your country." Suddenly it was night. Without warning we drank too much beer. The fat lemons in the backyard blew up. *Wicky wicky* went the sinister, relentless oil derricks. The TV was on but nobody was watching. We must have wanted *something*.

In the morning Ed said to come into the kitchen. He opened the freezer. "Ants," he said. There was a line of ants coming from under the refrigerator, up the metal side, then into the freezer. There were crushed bodies along the edge of the door, a chain of smudges, and live ants following in a thin black stream. "And look here," Ed said. In the freezer there were thousands of dead ants. The shelves of the door and the compartments where you put cans of concentrated orange juice were entirely filled with their tiny shriveled husks, like poppy seeds, a handful of black spores. "They freeze to death. Every day I clean them out, and overnight it fills up again. Tim put some fish in here that he caught in Mexico. Maybe that's what it is." It was impossible to determine where exactly the ants came from. They seemed to materialize beneath the refrigerator, through a crack in the floor, maybe, or else they lived in the bowels of the machine itself, nesting there, laying eggs amid the coils and insulated wiring. Nor was it possible to stop them with ant traps, roach powder, boric acid. Each day they appeared, died, were sponged away, and appeared again. How good it must have smelled in there! How simple to follow that trail towards fish blood and plastic vaporous in the freezing darkness, a vein, a living highway, the path to the miniature elephant's graveyard.

Standing in the back door sucking the odor of fish from an ice cube you watch the decaying lemons and oranges preparing for the miraculous leap, the big jump back to the branches, the resurrection from the grass. The earth is an imperfect sphere revolving beneath your feet and just maybe you grow out of the earth like a lemon tree. Maybe the cracks in the driveway are the first delicate ruptures in the shell, tracings like the veins of a leaf, the egg boiled too long, leaking a spume of albumen, the absences of an infant's skull, blood, the yolk, the golden heart-shaped leaves of the gingko. That archangel blossoms into a spectacular crimson flower and falls again into the sea. The sea. The fall. Wind in the branches of the lemon tree. It is winter in Southern California. Los Angeles seethes within its aura of dust and smoke and toxic particles, full of heat and rage as the night is full of furious electrons. On Signal Hill the oil wells move relentlessly like Tinkertoy wrenches in the distance, insomniacs crucified in the white glare of spotlights, desperate machines saying *nothing, nothing, nothing.*

Yellowknife

A Cree elder told me how a man gone Windigo "had been asking his own brother how it was in a nearby beaver lodge. . . in the lodge! Because he saw his brother as a fat beaver and he wanted to eat him."

—Howard Norman, *Cree Windigo Tales and Journeys*

Late that day we stopped to help a family of Indians in a big red Chevy, the first car in hours, out of gas by the side of the road. This far north, Athabasca, Slave, and Swampy Cree Indians mix with Inuit or Eskimo, the pure Mongolian features of the young daughter who smiles shyly and plays peekaboo with Charlie while the father uses a length of hose as a siphon, squatting on his heels, spitting out mouthfuls of gas until it flows smoothly. Nobody says much, even Charlie doesn't talk. We stand around slapping mosquitoes until the jerry can is full and he thanks us and wanders back to his family, hidden in the backseat, smiling and nodding stiffly, like dolls, as he jumps in and drives off into the dusk. "It started right up," Charlie said. "They weren't out of gas at all." According to the Cree, the Windigo roams this wilderness in disguise—the Trails-End-at-Shivering Windigo, the Childhood Foxes Windigo, the Echoing Moth Windigo—swimming glacial lakes in seconds, freezing the heart with hysterical exhalations, bringing famine, hunger, and death. That night we crossed into the Northwest Territories and camped along the Hay River where a wild waterfall fell two hundred feet into the gorge. The air was filled with the torrent's crashing surge and sheets of mist that left us unable to speak, just staring up the canyon of the Hay River, winding off through scrubwood and muskeg wastes towards the Great Slave Lake, nothing but wilderness for hundreds of miles, nothing but desolation until Yellowknife, and nothing there but the Windigo, though we didn't know it then. We climbed back up from the falls in the glow of midnight sun. We ate hot dogs and Jiffy Pop in a hurry, fell asleep uneasily on ground gnarled with roots, the earth's fingers clutching our arms and legs, struggling to pull us under, to drag us down into the rocky soil.

This is something that happened on the Mackenzie Highway. One day two Americans were driving north when a young girl cried out to them for help. She stood next to a big red Chevy. When the Americans stopped to see what was wrong the girl's family jumped out and captured them, and tied them with cords and thongs. The Americans saw nothing and yet her family was there—they had conjured themselves to look like trees! "Why have you tricked us like this?" the Americans asked. The little girl said: "We did not wish to. We also are captives." Then a strange voice spoke: "You are my prisoners." There was no one there, and yet something spoke—a voice like winter wind! Then the Americans understood—it was the Red-Chevy Windigo! "I will take you to my home in Yellowknife. Get in." So they all got into the car, and the Red-Chevy Windigo began to fly high above the ground. They flew over the swampy forest extending to the horizons. They flew over the home of the moose and the beaver and the lakes full of arctic char. And they crossed the fearful Mackenzie River, past Fort Providence, along the Great Slave Lake, where the trees get small before fading off into tundra. They came to a city on the northern shore of the lake, a city with tall buildings and neon signs, with gas stations and heavy traffic and a McDonald's—like a suburb whose nearest neighbor was five hundred miles south. There were video games and four-wheel-drive vehicles! "This is my home," the Windigo said. "This is Yellowknife." In Yellowknife the Windigo left the Americans at the Motel 6. They ate Kentucky Fried Chicken and drank cold beer. In the evening the Americans drank whiskey at the Klondike Bar with gold miners and oil roughnecks. The streets of Yellowknife were filled with Eskimos and Indians who sat on the stairs of the city hall or the library, public buildings so they couldn't be evicted, drunk, or drinking white port, or staggering down the sidewalks, or tumbling into the gutter. The Americans stayed three days, drinking beer, depressed, watching TV cabled in from Detroit. They saw three shows with Dick Van Patten in one morning! Their Colonel Sanders piggy banks came to life and danced in front of the screen! They cried out to the marten and to the badger and the she-weasel, but no one came to release them. It happened that one day three ravens were passing by and saw the Americans and understood what had befallen them. The eldest raven said: "Look how piteously they cry out. They think they are tied down by fierce enemies, but the Windigo comes from within. Even in the barren lands he may make a place his own." Then the old raven's son said: "They don't understand that they are prisoners of their own hearts!" Then the ravens laughed and flew away. That was how it happened.

In the morning we broke camp for the last leg north. The Mackenzie was turgid, grey, compulsive, a timber wolf's river. The trees thinned and lichen-covered rocks poked up among wildflowers in the bogs and stagnant lakes. As we approached Yellowknife we somehow knew what to expect—the shadows of office buildings on the lake, blocks of prefab houses, the jingle of the player piano from Shakey's, the 7-11.

To kill a Windigo you must melt its heart of ice. This far north it seemed unlikely.

The Windigo laughed as we pulled into the Motel 6, howled like the wind as we left three days later, and all the way back down the heart of the continent.

The Red-Chevy Windigo has many names.

Coal Miner

Into the rain-washed evening white
with evangelical fury a man walks silently, raccoon-eyed, white-

irised, neck and arms black
with coal dust. He is a coal miner. Every day he sports this black

mineral rime like a cheap suit—Pennsylvania
sharkskin, the men say. At this hour the valleys of Pennsylvania

are full of jet-black men rising
from the anthracite seams as the harvest moon rises

like a jack-o'-lantern over the hills.
Now they drive home through the broken jawbone hills

in rusted red and blue
pickup trucks, too fast, tired and hungry and lost in the blue

country radio music—Johnny Paycheck's
"Take This Job and Shove It," which they would except for the money.

The man is a coal miner. Every day he rises
to descend. But now it is evening, and he smiles as he clears the rise

of the last ridge before home—
and now he is home and the smell of dinner greets him, home

as the Big Dipper rises
cruciform, and sparks shoot from the chimney, and wood smoke rises,

and fireflies rise,
and coal dust, milkweed, fog in the hollows—all things rise

to the last light.

Capitalist Poem #25

This is the dichotomy: on the one hand something from childhood. For instance, well—Superman. That is: more powerful than a locomotive . . . ; faster than a speeding . . . ; able to—(this is it)—change the course of mighty rivers. Like the Grand Coulee Dam. And people come from all around to see it, the largest tourist attraction in the Pacific Northwest, families from Seattle, Portland, all the way from Bismarck, North Dakota. And FDR created the CCC, which hired Woody Guthrie to come on up and write some songs about the boys involved in the electrification project, a great building and a damming and a tearing down of trees along the sinuous Columbia choked with logs. And Teddy Roosevelt created the National Parks so you could camp next to the family playing Scrabble in their Winnebago at a reservoir in Utah. And it was Thomas Jefferson who sent out Lewis and Clark in the first place, along the Missouri and across the mountains, and down the same Columbia to the sea. It's a sort of dialectic. Youth and maturity. Man against nature. Childhood or a motorboat in Utah: that's the dichotomy.

As far as I'm concerned, just about anything from TV was a more significant cultural phenomenon of the 60's than Vietnam. "The Flintstones," or "Mission: Impossible," or "Lost in Space." I could tell you things about "Lost in Space" you wouldn't believe. The carrot creatures crying "Moisture! Moisture!" The music that signals the invisible bog monster's approach. Uncle Angus covered with tendrils. I don't even know which are real episodes and which ones I made up anymore. I could tell you about the Baltimore Orioles. Roster moves, statistics, a twi-night doubleheader in August when the hot wind curls over the top of the bleachers and Eddie Murray wins the first game with a two-run double in the 8th. Between games the lines for beer and nachos are filled with laughing, smiling people exchanging jokes, weighing the season's prospects, savoring the victory. The second game is a pitching duel, scoreless through nine, until Jim Palmer tires and gives up a run in the top of the 10th and leaves to a standing ovation. As the Orioles come to bat the crowd hums with energy, excited but not at all nervous, certain of victory in fact, because this is the magic summer of 1979 and fate is on the side of Baltimore. Inevitably, the Orioles get two men on, and, with two out, Eddie Murray comes to the plate. Ed and Charlie and I are up screaming, Memorial Stadium chants in unison—"Edd-ie, Edd-ie, Edd-ie"—and when Eddie swings at a 1-1 pitch we know it's gone even before the ball rockets off his bat in a tremendous arc, moving slowly and even gently through the air, perfectly visible, stage-lit against the deep green of the grass, the right fielder not moving, just turning his head to watch it go, and it's like the perfect arc of youth, a constellation made up of baseball, booze, girls and loud music, and even at 19 or 22 when the stars have shifted slightly to malt liquor, loud music, women, vandalism and sports in general, that ball is still rising, old age and death are impossibly remote, and anyway those images of hooded figures and the grim reaper with his scythe are impossibly outdated, and now death is a giant incarnation of Fred Flintstone, impossibly huge, skewering passersby on cocktail swords like giggling olives, and he roams the outfield shagging flies, pulling the ball out of the sky in mid-flight, laughing loud as a hyena in the yellow and black-spotted skin he wears like a bathrobe, and even Eddie Murray can't hit one beyond his reach as he lopes across the grass, immense and belligerent and well intentioned, like America, clubbing his friend Barney Rubble on the head, and even if he were to slip, just once, on loose gravel near the warning track, say, we know the laws of physics, we know the parabola must start downward somewhere, and in the split second it takes to react to the home run you see that this is life, a luminous rise and a steady, frictional wearing down, a curve disintegrating in the sure pull of gravity, Eddie Murray dropping his bat and starting the slow trot around the bases, the crowd coming to its feet, the ball finally crashing into the bull pen.

And you're rising up with a great emotional surge swelling inside you. You're standing on the aluminum bench with Ed and Charlie stamping your feet. You're waving your arms wildly in the air. You're looking up, past the glowing towers of lights, at the floodlit sky. You're yelling like there's no tomorrow.

Two

Dust

I thought about the dust
I thought about the sand
I thought about the people
and I thought about the land ©
—Woody Guthrie

The Genius of Industry

Lay me on an anvil, O God.
Beat me and hammer me into a crowbar.
—Carl Sandburg

Lost in the Wilderness,

crouched in the underbrush as the flames approached,
the rattle of muskets mingling with the cries of the wounded
caught in the creeping wildfires and burned to death,

the blindness of days
pushing further into that miasma of killing,

the men were left with little to ponder
but the character of their new Commanding General,
Ulysses S. Grant.

Surely, so the talk went
in the camp of the 5th Michigan
and the 9th New Hampshire, the 21st Ohio
and Indiana's famous Iron Brigade,
surely he would retreat.
Faced with this indecisive firefight,
thickets of scrub oak in hidden gulches,
heavy losses on both sides,
the danger of a sudden reversal
as at Chancellorsville,

surely Grant would retreat
like all the others—
McClellan and Burnside, Hooker and Pope—
move back to Washington and resupply,
prepare to try again next month, or next season,
or next spring. It was only common sense.

And in the days and weeks that followed—

cold marches through the woods of Virginia,
the Bloody Angle of Spotsylvania,
the two armies locked together day and night,
grinding the life from each other
like implacable lovers—

as the men discovered that Grant would not retreat,
that Grant meant relentless battle,

it could be said that America
discovered its particular genius:
getting down to business.

As personified in Sam Grant,
a smallish, red-bearded man
seated beneath an oak tree in a dirty uniform
whittling a stick into smaller
and smaller pieces, making nothing,
it was a genius for death.
In that final struggle of the war,
a continual, year-long skirmish from the Wilderness
to its conclusion, a sort of square dance where
the partners rushed out and fired
round after round
from twenty paces beneath a bright sun,
new men stepping up
to take the place of the fallen
while the caller whistled out directions,
do-si-do and promenade,
it was Grant who called the tune, relentlessly
and without mercy. It took the North
four years for Lincoln to find Grant,
hidden away in the heartland
getting drunk and winning battles,
and bring him east to end it.

I need this man, old bloody-handed Abe said.
He knows how to fight. He knew
that victory meant *getting down to*
the job at hand; meant relentless pressure;
meant "the maximization of the numerical advantage
and the superior productive capacity of the North."
Most of all, he knew that victory meant death,
a new, fully modern kind of death,
an industrialized democracy of killing
in the muddy siege works and trenches around Petersburg,
at the fords along the Pamunkey and the Rappahannock,
in the slaughter of Cold Harbor
and the crossroads at Five Forks,
the last footrace with Lee's starving men
ending finally beneath the dogwoods of Appomattox
in the victory not so much of one general,
or even one army, as of a particular vision of America,
an ideology just coming into its own.

Across the distance of a century
we can see that this is what matters,
not so much the man himself
as what he signifies—though Grant
is so perfectly American,
his pragmatic strength and paradoxical weaknesses,
the love of booze and horses and cheap cigars.
Ulysses Grant was to warfare
what Henry Ford was to the automobile.
And as the military purists
even today resent Grant's lack of subtlety,
the absence of Napoleonic finesse,
we imagine the dismay
of the fine craftsmen of the Old World,
laboring over their hand-tooled
products, self-righteous and scornful

of the Model T's rolling off the assembly line,
and Ford thinking *fuck them*
I want to rule the world.
As after the war Grant's lieutenants,
Sherman and Sheridan, scoured the West
turning bad Indians into good ones, taming
the wilderness, making the world safe for democracy;
thus was Montana made safe for the Great Northern Railroad,
immigrants conned into settling by such extravagant claims
that the Dakotas came to be known as "Jay Cooke's Banana Belt";
thus the plains were settled and cities arose in the desert;
thus were cartels born; thus were bubbles burst;
thus General Motors and the rubber industry
got together with John D. Rockefeller
to purchase the Los Angeles interurban transport system,
one of the most modern and extensive in the country,
and dismantled it, as a public service, so that
the automobile—"the future of America"—
should have less disruptive competition,
in the process making millions for themselves at the expense
of the general public, which after all is the definition
of a great Capitalist. And o the beautiful freeways,
the Santa Monica and the Long Beach and the San Diego!
Phoenix and Los Angeles as much a part of it
as Detroit or Pittsburgh with their
smelters and rolling mills and slag heaps,
strip mining in West Virginia
and strings of motels like diamonds in the desert
outside Gallup, New Mexico,
everything a product of the cultural assembly line.
Because it wasn't so much the machines themselves—
though the power of those cogs and wheels
to dehumanize the average Joe
should not be underestimated—
as it was a new idiom,
a new pace to American life, an endless refinement

down to some replicable pattern,
an industrialized essence,
as William Carlos Williams
hammered out language, manufacturing a poetry
pure as circuit boards. A rhythm,
waves lapping the shore of Lake Michigan
as you head south along the Drive, south
into the industrial belt,
Hammond, Gary, East Chicago,
the gas jets of the refineries, smokestacks gushing steam,
a million naked bulbs in the white glow
of phosphorus, the rumble of machinery,
sky bruised orange by the roar of production.
Or sailing up the Mississippi after dusk
between banks alive with petroleum plants,
the cabled towers of relay stations
and chemical-storage facilities,
bright as day all night and
all the way up to Baton Rouge
where the giant snake-headed hoses
load corn into the deep holds of the freighter,
a mountain of chipped yellow grain,
and the fine, powdery residue
turning the cranes
and all the sailors white, dust—
corn dust—that gums your eyes shut,
an overpowering taste
that will linger all the way to Veracruz.

That afternoon, after loading, the ship
puts about and runs south, pale as talcum,
nestling deep into the water with its new weight.

By day the riverbanks are Amazonian.
The warehouses and lading bays
without their blinding electrical eyes

seem inconsequential, lost against the swampy horizon,
Louisiana sweeping past hour by hour
as you crouch hammering rust from the hull,

hearing the waters part before you,
the intonations of the mallets
on the thick steel plates, a dull ringing

of calloused hands hammering steadily
beneath the white sun while each stroke
raises a cloud of rust chips into your face

and the dragonflies settle by the hundreds
to bask on the hot metal of the deck
and then rise again at each reverberation,

rising and falling to the beat of the hammers,
the whole insect mass like an emerald
and turquoise lung, rising and falling,

the pulse of a primordial engine.

The Cult of the Individual

1

He was magnificently alone.

There was a light
in the shallows
where the river

widened,

deer moving
at the water's edge.

He was alone
with the buffalo

which roamed those woods then,
the greennesses roiling up towards the Cumberland Gap,

purple-edged,
at dusk. The rocks,

the streams and
the very rivers were his companions.
He was

Daniel Boone in old Kentucky. He was

Jim Skinner, scout and trailblazer,
Lewis and Clark crossing the Rockies,

Sam Houston,
    Governor of Texas,
Senator and Presidential candidate,
who ran away to live with the Cherokees
    at age sixteen.

He was
   the bearded prospector
wandering into town on his mule after
discovering uranium near Coaldale, Nevada—
   a substance which

pulses with strange green light
and tastes as sweet as Juicyfruit gum!

Or the trail hand Charlie Siringo.

Or Bill Pickett,
   the black cowboy
who bit the lips of steers, hanging on
like a bulldog to bring them into submission,
   breaking them in,

bending animal nature to one man's will.

And if you've seen
   smiling monkeys
in black cowboy hats and tiny six-shooters
riding trained dogs at the Granddaddy of Them All,
   the Cheyenne Rodeo,

and Fess Parker
   teaching otters how
to read by the light of a coal-oil lamp,
or whatever it is he does, or did,
   as *Daniel Boone*

on TV—so what?

They were magnificent in their isolation.

2

23rd August.

Set out this morning very early.
I walked on shore and killed a fat buck.
J. Fields sent out to hunt; came to the boat
and informed that he had killed a buffalo
in the plain ahead.

                    In the next bend
two elk swam the river . . .

R. Fields came up with the horses
and brought two deer.

Several prairie wolves seen today.
Saw elk standing on the sand bar.

The wind

blew hard and raised the sands off the bar
in such clouds that we could scarcely see.
This sand,
            being fine and very light,
stuck to everything it touched,

and in the plain for half a mile—
the distance I was out—

every spire of grass was covered with sand or dirt. . . .

*For Meriwether Lewis, twenty-nine and Captain of the Corps of Discovery,
the journey of the Lewis and Clark Expedition was a progression of carefully
measured days, a slow accumulation of detail. What is, to us, the greatest
American voyage, in all its richness, the discoveries of animals and birds,
rivers, mountain ranges, an unfenced continent, the epic herds and the sea
of grass, Lewis depicts in his journals as we might tell of a drive to a friend's*

*house in Connecticut—where the traffic was bad, stopping for coffee, meat
loaf and gravy for dinner. The slow cycle of the quotidian circumscribed
each day into a routine of making-do. Even to Lewis, though, there were
times of transcendence—a sequence of luminous hours like a string of pearls
unwinding; moments that reflect an essence, a distillation of a mythic
American past; minutes of pure, numinous grace.*

There is the day Lewis spends exploring the Great Falls of the Missouri alone.

About ten o'clock this morning
I took my gun and espontoon
and thought I would walk a few miles
to see where the rapids terminated. . . .

At the distance of about five miles
I arrived at a fall of about 19 feet.
This I named the Crooked Falls.
I should have returned from hence;
but, hearing a tremendous roaring above me,
I continued my route, and was rewarded—

    a cascade of about fifty feet perpendicular,
stretching across the river side to side,
at least a quarter of a mile. The water
descends in one even sheet to the bottom,
where, dashing against the rocks,
    it rises into foaming billows of great height
and rapidly glides away,
               hissing, flashing and sparkling.

Below this fall,
        on a beautiful little island,
well timbered, in a cottonwood tree,
an eagle has built her nest. A more inaccessible spot
she could not have found,
        I believe,
for neither man nor beast dare pass those gulfs
which separate her domain from the shore.

I determined to ascend the hill behind me,
which promised a fine prospect; nor was I disappointed.
From hence I overlooked a most beautiful and extensive plain
reaching from the river
    to the snow-clad base of the mountains.
In these plains, and more particularly
in the valley just below me,
immense herds of buffalo are feeding.
           I also observed the Missouri,
stretching its meandering course to the south,
filled to its even and grassy brim,
a smooth and unruffled sheet of water nearly a mile in width,
bearing on its watery bosom
vast flocks of geese.

I thought it would be well
to kill a buffalo and leave him
until my return from the river.
           Under this impression
I selected a fat buffalo and shot him,
very well, through the lungs.

While I was gazing at the poor animal,
      and having entirely forgotten
to reload my rifle,
      a large Grizzly bear
had perceived and crept on me within twenty paces
before I discovered him.

It was an open and level plain, not a bush within miles.

I decided to face about and walk slowly away,
but I had no sooner turned around than he pitched at me, open-
    mouthed.
I ran hastily into the water, about waist deep,
and presented the point of my espontoon—
           the moment

I put myself in the attitude of defense,
he suddenly wheeled about as if frightened
and retreated with great precipitation.
I saw him run about three miles before he disappeared
in the woods along Medicine River. So it was;
    and I felt myself not a little gratified
that he had declined combat.
My gun reloaded, I felt confidence once more
        in my strength.

I now determined to return,
having by my estimate about 12 miles to walk.
My direction led me directly to an animal
that I at first suspected was a wolf. But,
                            on nearer approach
its color was brownish-yellow. It was standing
near its burrow,
                and when I came up it crouched
down like a cat and scurried to shelter.
It now seemed to me that all the beasts of the neighborhood
had made a league to destroy me,
for I had not gone 300 yards from the burrow of the tiger cat,
    before three bull buffalo
separated from the rest of their herd
and ran full speed toward me.
                            However,
I altered my path to meet them,
and at a certain distance they halted, before
retreating.
            I then continued my route homeward,
passed the buffalo which I had earlier killed,
but did not think it prudent to remain
all night at this place, which, really,
from the succession of curious adventures,
wore the impression on my mind of enchantment.

    At some times,
        for a moment,

I thought it might be a dream,

                          but the prickly pears
which pierced my feet convinced me I was awake.

It was some time after dark before I returned to the party.
I found them extremely uneasy for my safety.
I felt myself much fatigued, but ate a hearty supper
and took a good night's rest. The weather being warm,
I had left my leather overcoat

and had worn only a yellow flannel one.

The date was June 14th, 1805.

3

There is a terrible loneliness in America, in its vast empty spaces, its dis-
tances and recesses, its prairies and deserts and its endlessly retreating
mountain ranges: the Medicine Bow and the Rattlesnake Hills, the Wind
River Range, the Tetons and the Bitterroots, the San Juans and the Sangre
de Cristo Mountains. There is a loneliness in Kalispell and Baltimore, the
towns of Utah and Ohio alike, the anthracite country of Pennsylvania and
the iron towns of Minnesota, a loneliness lingering like the final steel-guitar
note that quavers into silence at the Texan Bar in Rifle, Colorado, as the song
ends and the bar empties down to the last red-eyed customer dancing a tall-
neck bottle of beer across the floor to the tune of some unnamable sorrow.
Or the scent of spring rain in Duck, North Carolina, squalls coming off the
grey and silver sea to the beach, wracked by waves, where an old black man
pulls bluefish one after another from the surf and drops them in a yellow
bucket. Or the shadows of heat waves thrown across a wall in Chicago,
convection currents, where the cold presses against the window and the
radiator throws out warmth, like wind thrashing winter wheat, an active
force visible only through its consequences—the shaken grain, the delicate
smoke-like shadows, spirals of dust rising in blue, incandescent light.

Today the city of Great Falls, Montana, occupies that bend of the Missouri,
and the falls themselves have been mostly lost to damming and flood

control. Great Falls is the second-largest city in Montana, and the site of the annual State Fair, where you can eat a corn dog and examine the latest farm machinery and prize bulls as big as small cars; visit the 4-H Club and the Future Farmers' exhibit on toxic prairie weeds and the local Democratic Party booth with photos of cattle and LBJ; buy rattlesnake boots and chew on good beef jerky; drink the freshest glass of milk you ever tasted in the dairy barn or wander the Blue Ribbon food hall with its ranks of glass cases—pickled onions and radishes and baby carrots, corn bread and biscuits and johnny cakes, peach and apricot preserves, mincemeat pie, elderberry wine—like a vast museum of Boy Scout dementia. It is a nice, quiet city, an overgrown town, really, with a strip of bars for hard-luck cowboys and blocks of houses with white picket fences, and if the plains of Montana are no longer a rolling wilderness of grasses dotted with herds of elk and antelope, they are still majestic, and crossing them on 12 or 89 is a beautiful journey.

And if the loneliness of the West doesn't find you in Great Falls, there is always another town, another grain elevator and empty siding, another day of driving. There is always Guthrie Center, Iowa, desolate in the sea of growth, nothing but corn, green hair waving, that fearful fertility. There is always Lakin, Kansas, and Panguitch, Utah, and Sanderson, Texas. There is always Enders, Nebraska, where I bought some hot dogs and a cold six-pack after a long day's drive, and a permit for the little campground by the reservoir, still and quiet under the trees, wind in the cottonwoods and tall pines, the rustling of reeds like calico dresses down by the water. The campground was empty except for me, empty parking spaces, a half-dozen trash barrels, rusty swings by the landing. I built a fire, sitting on a stump, watching the wood catch, watching ants caught by the flames on the hot stones, listening to the trees, the crackle of the branches—when the moment of lonely panic gripped me so fiercely I threw everything back in the car, loose hot dogs, the jumbled tent and sleeping bag, and hit the road spraying gravel, desperate to get out of Enders, to get someplace else, someplace with people, Imperial or McCook, all the way to Denver if necessary, anywhere but here. Anywhere but alone with these fields, these trees waving in the wind, this empty road and the sun going down. Anywhere but this gully with horses and dead trees, a collapsed barn on a hill, three blue silos in the distance.

I drove for twenty miles before calming, before turning back to Enders, to
the drowsy reservoir, the empty campground. I slept out, looking up at the
stars between the boles of the trees, listening to the insects and the grass.
I woke once in the middle of the night and the moon was gone, hidden by
fiery clouds, orange and silver, seams of coal burning way down, way down
deep, a fire in the mountain.

4

And Meriwether Lewis,
barely three years after his triumphant return,

proud Captain,
    hero to a nation,
Governor of the new Louisiana Territory,
saw invisible enemies in the tall grass and dark woods
    along the Natchez Trace,

saw a closing in beneath the canopy of ash and cypress,

saw the need
    to escape, fooling them—
the dangerous ones in the black grass—and so
one night near dawn he set the horses loose,
    whispering urgently

to the stallions galloping wildly through the half-light,

and when his companions went to find them
he shot himself in the heart with his pistol.

But the ball,
    entering at the chest
and exiting through his lower back, missed his heart—
demonstrating the fickleness of that muscle—
    and failed even

to strike his lungs
   or other vital organ.
Seeing his error, realizing that his friends would
return and tend his wound and heal him—
   watching him even more closely,

      perhaps tying his wrists,
no doubt keeping him away from the bottle—

he took matters further into his own hands.

And when the family
   in the neighboring cabin,
hearing his repeated screams, sent their son out
with a bowl of water for the famous Captain,
   the boy found him still alive,

sitting up in bed, carving himself with his hunting knife.

He was a blood-filled tree!
He was a human totem!

He was covered with delicate incisions, head to foot,

blood running
   rich and bright
like the Missouri and the Columbia and the Snake,
the Yellowstone and the Milk, the Musselshell and the Marias
   and the Salmon,

rivers he had discovered,
   or named, or mapped, or conquered,

and with his last breath
   he told the boy he had killed himself

to deny his enemies that pleasure.

Dust

Days, hours, minutes,
a hunger for the fruit of some dimly remembered past.

A man waiting for the bus with a vacuum cleaner.

Miles click by, trees, memories,
the reflective eyes of highway markers
in the darkness. The movie stops,
then starts again,
random images tumbling from the projector,
a newsreel out of control.

While crossing the reservation in Arizona a song from your childhood
comes on the radio in Navajo. The DJ's voice and singsong elocution,
jangling banjo wires, scattered English phrases embedded like ivory stones—
computer science class, Gatorade, the Lovesick Blues.

Great Falls and Guthrie Center.
Shiloh and Antietam.
Plymouth Rock and the Grand Coulee Dam.

Whatever list we choose will be inadequate:

apples, drops of water, sunlight's
shattered prismatic radiance.

Days measured out like cornmeal, or flour,
measured out like salt.

We keep waiting for the moment when everything comes together, the
revelation on the mountaintop, when the streams and rivers rush past,
growing out of our bodies like hair, veins and arteries flowing with lambent
energy, music, a kind of noise. . . . We're in Montana, standing and looking
up at the stars, the countless lights of the Big Sky, the vast plains rolling out
silently at our feet, the lights of the towns reflecting up from the prairie, the
secret lights, the web of roads, the whorl, the great matrix of America
revealed at last.

But it doesn't happen that way. Instead we pick up a hitchhiker named Ray, dirty and shirtless, tattooed, with a dog and a plastic garbage bag holding everything he owns. Near Pocatello we pass a giant dust cloud, yellow and red, stirred up by farm equipment, and a rainbow arches across the highway, and the canyon of the Snake River, a rainbow in the cloud of dust.

Silt and Rifle, Cortez and Alamosa, Empire and Grand Lake:
the mountain towns of Colorado.

The names of the towns are nothing
but sand carried down on the wind.

Language itself is just dust,
crystalline particles,
a blue snow descending in silence.

We can never hope to get it all down, never more than a suggestion, an essence, the string of pearls unwinding. The lumberjack who scales the tallest of trees with ease but slips again and again on the greased totem— antelope and owl, the eagle we intuitively understand to represent *Myths of the American Past*—and finally stands in the mud, looking up, past the carved pole, past the hills, to the sky, clouds moving against a depth of unimaginable blue, beyond *cerulean* and *indigo*, too clear for words, too pure, and feels within himself the stirring of a deep and abiding faith.

"What's the dog's name, Ray?" He doesn't have a name. *"What do you call him?"* Dog.

Memory, love, depiction, the words themselves
deny us, slip through our hands.

We drank six kinds of malt liquor.
We ate at McDonald's four times in one day.

You can drive from D.C. to L.A. in 48 hours
if you just average 60 mph, including stops.

The days retract like a telescope, images and words. The moment slips away. It never existed. The vision on the mountaintop never happened.

56

The stars are only two-dimensional, etched on the ceiling. The rivers that flowed from our bodies solidify into crowds of people pushing past, commuters heading home to the clustered suburbs, the towns of Connecticut and New Jersey.

It isn't Montana at all. It's New York City.

I'm standing in Grand Central Station,
looking up at the vaulted roof
painted with star charts and luminous constellations:

the fish, the hunter, the great bear.

It's Grand Central Station and the people
push around me, ambient, breaking on the rocks,
flooding the stairways and corridors.

It's Grand Central Station and I'm waiting for my lover,
waiting for the walk home through the hushed city,
cloaked and blanketed against winter—

snow is starting to fall, dark waves
driven down beneath the streetlights,
settling like the ash of memory.

Minutes, hours, miles, a childlike hunger for faith . . .

The crush of humanity surrounds us,
the animate hum, the giant clock ticking off seconds
like heartbeats reverberating through an immense marble hall.

Days measured out like salt.
Measured out like gold dust.

I'm waiting for Elizabeth.
I'm standing beneath the true American stars.
I'm looking up, in wonder.

About the Author

Campbell McGrath has traveled extensively throughout the United States, Europe, North Africa, Australia, and the Pacific. He has lived among the Umbandistas of Brazil and the Cargo Cultists of Vanuatu, in Melanesia. His many jobs have included that of a sailor, carpenter, stock car driver, and alligator wrestler. McGrath won the Academy of American Poets Prize in 1984, 1986, and 1987, and his series of poems "Five Sonnets for Joseph Cornell" was included in the 1989 *New Voices* anthology, published by Academy of American Poets Press. During 1988 and 1989 he taught creative writing in the New York City public schools. He presently lives in Chicago.

About the Book

Capitalism is composed in ITC Garamond. Garamond, named for the sixteenth-century French type designer Claude Garamond, was introduced in the United States by American Type Foundry in 1919, when their cutting, based on the *caractères de l'Université* of the Imprimerie Nationale, appeared. Many other versions were made for Linotype, Monotype, Intertype, Ludlow, and the Stempel foundry. The face has since been adapted for phototypesetting, CRT typesetting, and laser typesetting. The book was composed, designed, and produced by Kachergis Book Design of Pittsboro, North Carolina.